THE LOG CABIN QUILT

by Ellen Howard

illustrated by Ronald Himler

Holiday House/New York

Text copyright © 1996 by Ellen Howard
Illustrations copyright © 1996 by Ronald Himler
ALL RIGHTS RESERVED
Printed in the United States of America
Library of Congress Cataloging-in-Publication Data
Howard, Ellen.
The log cabin quilt / by Ellen Howard: illustrated by Ronald
Himler. — 1st ed.
p.   cm.
Summary: When Elvirey and her family move to a log cabin in the
Michigan woods, something even more important than Granny's quilt
pieces makes the new dwelling a home.
ISBN 0-8234-1247-4 (hc: alk. paper)
[1. Log cabins—Fiction. 2. Quilts—Fiction. 3. Grandmothers—
Fiction. 4. Family life—Fiction.] I. Himler, Ronald, ill.
II. Title.
PZ7.H83274Lo   1996   95-50888   CIP   AC
[E]—dc20
ISBN 0-8234-1336-5 (pbk.)

For Audrienne and Zachary, from their granny

My granny was a great one for quilting. She had this *big* flour sack full of scraps. Squares and triangles and diamonds and stripes, all colors. Soft shiny pieces from Mam's petticoats. Rough scratchy pieces from Pap's work pants. Calico, softened and faded with washings from Bub's old shirts and my hand-me-down dresses from Sis.

We brought that sack of quilting scraps from Carolina, all the way in the wagon to the woods of Michigan. That was after we'd laid our mam to rest in the old graveyard back home.

My pap never asked us did we want to stay or go. He just commenced to load the wagon. When I fetched Mam's things, her pictures and her books—"There ain't no room for suchlike," he said. It pained me something fierce to leave Mam's things behind.

But there was no leaving Granny's quilting scraps. She heaved the sack onto the seat and glared my pap right down. "I aim to set on it," she said.

So Pap strode out ahead of the horses. Mostly us younguns walked to save our teeth and bones. Granny rode, up on her sack, and I reckon *her* bones just rattled on that long and weary ride.

It was coming on winter when the wagon pulled up in the place Pap said was home. A clearing in the wood seemed no home to me, but I was glad to stop.

"Glory be!" said Granny.

Right off, Pap and Bub commenced to build the cabin. Soon the woods rang with the sound of their chopping. The clearing grew bigger as the trees were felled.

We camped beside a spring and made a stump our table. Granny huddled in the wagon and pieced on her quilts. Every night got colder, seemed to me.

The day the cabin roof went on was a day of jubilee. Sis and I chinked the log walls with mud and grass and moss.

"That'll keep out the wind, Elvirey," Pap said to me, and I felt the gladdest I had since home.

But he didn't smile. Pap never smiled these days.

We unpacked the wagon and carried in our goods. Pap helped Granny walk in.

"It'll soon feel like home," said Granny.

But it didn't. Even with the table scrubbed and the stools set around it, even with Granny in her rocker, piecing on a quilt, it didn't feel like home.

Mam had been a great one for flowers. When there were no flowers, she'd find a branch of berries to put into a jug. So, to pretty things a mite, I tied on my shawl and went to look for some.

There wasn't so much as a yellow leaf. The trees stood black and naked. I couldn't find a berry. I couldn't find a bud.

The wind was blowing. It made my ears ache. I went back empty-handed.

Nothing brightened the table. The walls of the cabin were bare. Granny's Bible was our only book. It didn't feel like home.

In the morning, Pap went hunting.

"We need meat for winter," he said.

I could see by Bub's face he longed to go too.

But, "Look after your sisters and Gran," Pap said. "I'll be home afore dark."

He wasn't.

It was a good, big fireplace that Pap had made. The fire burned high and bright.

Still, the cabin was cold. Outside we could hear the crying wind. We could feel the darkness press close to the door. We did not speak of Pap, alone in the woods. We never spoke of Mam.

The cold shivered my back, though my cheeks turned red, I sat so near the fire.

I scorched my dress, but Granny didn't scold.

She hunched in her chair, her shawl on her head, stretching her hands to the fire. I saw she wasn't piecing, as she always did of an evening. My stomach went queer to see her empty hands.

"Can I fetch you your scrap sack, Granny?" I said.

Granny didn't answer.

"Bub," I said. "Put more wood on the fire. I reckon Granny's cold."

"Elvirey, the fire don't need no wood," he said. "It ain't the *fire's* at fault. It's these walls let the wind blow through."

"We chinked 'em good," I said.

"Morning comes, we'll chink 'em again," Sis said, shivering in her coat. " 'Pears the chinks didn't hold."

I *knew* we had chinked those logs real tight. I jumped right up to look.

What I saw was a wonder to me. The mud chinks had frozen, and some had pushed out. When I held my hand to a crack, I could feel the wind blow in.

And something else. Something fine and white that sifted like sugar between the logs. I touched it and felt its cold.

"Snow," said Bub.

I ran to the door and pulled it open. Outside the darkness swirled with cold. Cold I could see and feel and taste. Back home, it was never so cold.

"Shet that door," said Bub.

I shut the door. My teeth chattered so's I couldn't speak. I crept back to the fire.

At Granny's knee, I sat on my stool. I felt her hand on my hair. When I turned my head up to look at her face, I saw by her eyes she was thinking of Pap. Pap in the snow. I couldn't bear what I saw in her eyes.

I fetched the quilting scraps.

They spilled into the firelight like scraps of memory. Red and yellow and blue and green. Rough and smooth. Bright and faded. Soft and stiff. All the pieces of our family's life, scattered on the floor.

I gathered up a handful of scraps and ran to stuff them in a crack.

"No need to wait for mornin'," I said. "We can chink the walls right now."

I could feel the others watch me as I pushed the scraps into the cracks, brushing away the snow. Each time, a little wind was stilled. A bit of cold was warmed.

Then I heard the swish of Sis's skirts. I heard Bub's boots on the floor. While I chinked the low cracks, they chinked the high. Together, we went around the walls, making the cabin tight.

I heard the creak of Granny's chair. I turned to look at her face. It was working in the firelight, as though she might commence to cry.

Then I saw that Granny was laughing!

"It's a log cabin quilt!" she cried.

Sis and I slept in Granny's bed that night, pulled as near to the fire as we dared. I was warm in the bed, with Sis on one side and Granny on the other. But before I could sleep, I said a prayer.

"Please rest Mam's soul, and bring Pap home again."

A thumping at the door woke me. As I sat up in bed, I saw Sis at the hearth, baking our breakfast bread. Granny, in her rocker, held her Bible in her lap. Bub pulled open the door.

A beam of sunlight, as sharp as the air, pierced the dusk of the cabin. On the threshhold swayed Pap. He looked like to drop, but behind him, he'd dragged home a deer.

"Pap!" I cried, tumbling out of bed.

"Pap!" cried Bub and Sis.

Granny breathed, "Son."

Bub lowered Pap's travois poles down to the ground and helped him to the fire. His eyebrows and beard were frosted with snow. His clothes were stiff with cold.

"Set you down here," Granny said, giving up her chair.

When he'd ceased to shiver, Pap told of his night, warmed by the carcass of the deer in a hollow beneath a log. He drank his coffee as he told. His fingers curved 'round the warmth of the cup as though they'd never leave it.

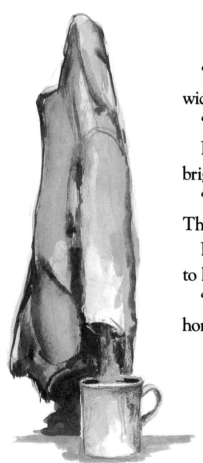

"It's good to be home," he said, looking about. Then his eyes opened wide.

"What in thunderation?" he said.

In the morning's light, the colors of the quilt scraps made the cabin bright.

"Elvirey thought of it, Pap," Sis said. "Our chinking froze and fell out. Then Elvirey thought of Gran's quiltin' scraps . . ."

I was holding my breath, watching Pap's face. Something was happening to his eyes, a softening, a crinkling, a *smile*.

"Your mam would be proud," Pap said to me. "The place is downright homey."

Of a sudden, I saw that Pap spoke the truth. The cabin did feel like home. But it wasn't the quilt scraps, it was Mam's name said out loud that made our cabin home.

"Elvirey!" Pap said, slapping his knee. "Elvirey, you do beat all!"